RESCUING THE ECONOMY
FROM THE GREAT RECESSION

The first and most fundamental task the Administration faced when President Obama took office was to rescue an economy in freefall. In November 2008, employment was declining at a rate of more than half a million jobs per month, and credit markets were stretched almost to the breaking point. As the economy entered 2009, the decline accelerated, with job loss in January reaching almost three-quarters of a million. The President responded by working with Congress to take unprecedented actions. These steps, together with measures taken by the Federal Reserve and other financial regulators, have succeeded in stabilizing the economy and beginning the process of healing a severely shaken economic and financial system. But much work remains. With high unemployment and continued job losses, it is clear that recovery must remain the key focus of 2010.

AN ECONOMY IN FREEFALL

According to the National Bureau of Economic Research, the United States entered a recession in December 2007. Unlike most postwar recessions, this downturn was not caused by tight monetary policy aimed at curbing inflation. Although economists will surely analyze this downturn extensively in the years to come, there is widespread consensus that its central precipitating factor was a boom and bust in asset prices, especially house prices. The boom was fueled in part by irresponsible and in some cases predatory lending practices, risky investment strategies, faulty credit ratings, and lax regulation. When the boom ended, the result was widespread defaults and crippling blows to key financial institutions, magnifying the decline in house prices and causing enormous spillovers to the remainder of the economy.

The Run-Up to the Recession

The rise in house prices during the boom was remarkable. As Figure 2-1 shows, real house prices almost doubled between 1997 and 2006. By 2006, they were more than 50 percent above the highest level they had reached in the 20th century.

Figure 2-1
House Prices Adjusted for Inflation

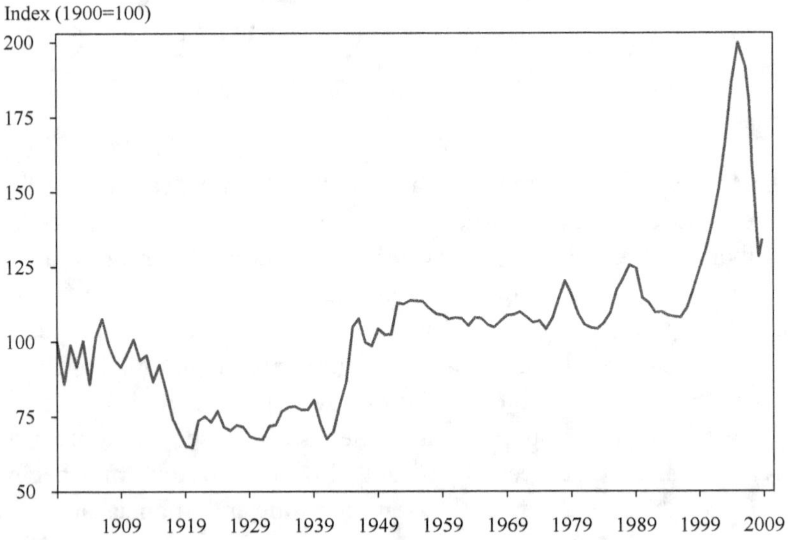

Index (1900=100)

Sources: Shiller (2005); recent data from http://www.econ.yale.edu/~shiller/data/Fig2-1.xls.

Stock prices also rose rapidly. The Standard and Poor's (S&P) 500, for example, rose 101 percent between its low in 2002 and its high in 2007. That rise, though dramatic, was not unprecedented. Indeed, in the five years before its peak in March 2000, during the "tech bubble," the S&P 500 rose 205 percent, while the more technology-focused NASDAQ index rose 506 percent.

The run-up in asset prices was associated with a surge in construction and consumer spending. Residential construction rose sharply as developers responded to the increase in housing demand. From the fourth quarter of 2001 to the fourth quarter of 2005, the residential investment component of real GDP rose at an average annual rate of nearly 8 percent. Similarly, consumers responded to the increases in the value of their assets by continuing to spend freely. Saving rates, which had been declining since the early 1980s, fell to about 2 percent during the two years before the recession. This spending was facilitated by low interest rates and easy credit, with household borrowing rising faster than incomes.

The Downturn

House prices began to drop in some markets in 2006, and then nationally beginning in 2007. This process was gradual at first, with prices measured using the LoanPerformance house price index declining just 3½ percent nationally between January and June 2007. Lenders had lent aggressively during the boom, often providing mortgages whose soundness hinged on continued house price appreciation. As a result, the comparatively modest decline in house prices threatened large losses on subprime residential mortgages (the riskiest class of mortgages), as well as on the slightly higher-quality "Alt-A" mortgages. As the availability of mortgage credit tightened, the downward pressure on real estate prices intensified. National house prices declined 6 percent between June and December 2007.

The negative feedback between credit availability and the housing market weighed on household and business confidence, restraining consumer spending and business investment. Although residential construction led the slowdown in real activity through 2007, by early 2008 outlays for consumer goods and services and business equipment and software had decelerated sharply, and total employment was beginning to decline. Real gross domestic product (GDP) fell slightly in the first quarter of 2008.

In February 2008, Congress passed a temporary tax cut. Figure 2-2 shows real after-tax (or disposable) income and consumer spending before and after rebate checks were issued. Consumption was maintained despite a tremendous decline in household wealth over the same period. Total household and nonprofit net worth declined 9.1 percent between June 2007 and June 2008. Microeconomic studies of consumer behavior in this episode confirm the role of the tax rebate in maintaining spending (Broda and Parker 2008; Sahm, Shapiro, and Slemrod 2009). The fact that real GDP reversed course and grew in the second quarter of 2008 is further tribute to the helpfulness of the policy. But, in part because of the lack of robust, sustained stimulus, growth did not continue.

Financial institutions had invested heavily in assets whose values were tied to the value of mortgages. For many reasons—the opacity of the instruments, the complexity of financial institutions' balance sheets and their "off-balance-sheet" exposures, the failure of credit-rating agencies to accurately identify the riskiness of the assets, and poor regulatory oversight—the extent of the institutions' exposure to mortgage default risk was obscured. When mortgage defaults rose, the result was unexpectedly large losses to many financial institutions.

In the fall of 2008, the nature of the downturn changed dramatically. More rapid declines in asset prices generated further loss of confidence in the ability of some of the world's largest financial institutions to honor

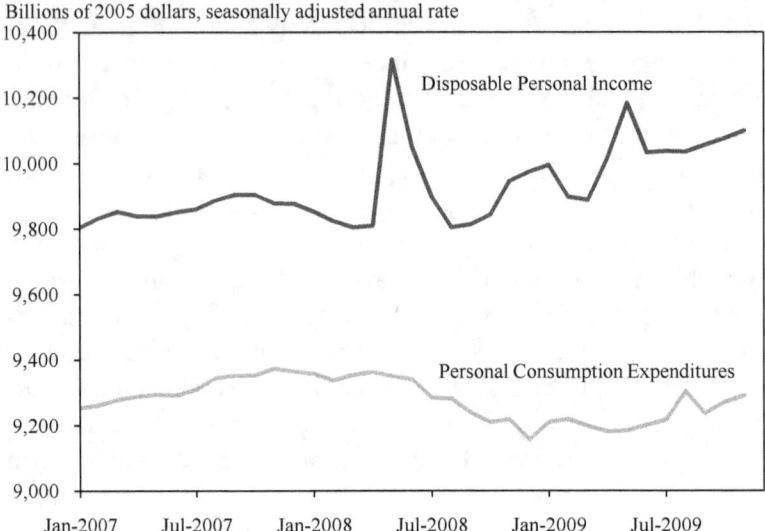

Figure 2-2
Income and Consumption Around the 2008 Tax Rebate

Billions of 2005 dollars, seasonally adjusted annual rate

Disposable Personal Income

Personal Consumption Expenditures

Sources: Department of Commerce (Bureau of Economic Analysis), National Income and Product Accounts Table 2.6, line 30, and Table 2.8.6, line 1.

their obligations. In September, the Lehman Brothers investment bank declared bankruptcy, and other large financial firms (including American International Group, Washington Mutual, and Merrill Lynch) were forced to seek government aid or to merge with stronger institutions. What followed was a rush to liquidity and a cascading of retrenchment that had many of the features of a classic financial panic.

Risk spreads shot up to extraordinary levels. Figure 2-3 shows both the TED spread and Moody's BAA-AAA spread. The TED spread is the difference between the rate on short-term loans among banks and a safe short-term Treasury interest rate. The BAA-AAA spread is the difference between the interest rates on high-grade and medium-grade corporate bonds. Both spreads rose dramatically during the heart of the panic. Indeed, one way to put the spike in the BAA-AAA spread in perspective is to note that the same spread barely moved during the Great Crash of the stock market in 1929, and rose by only about half as much during the first wave of banking panics in 1930 as it did in the fall of 2008.

The same loss of confidence shown by the rise in credit spreads translated into declining asset prices of all sorts. The S&P 500 declined 29 percent in the second half of 2008. Real house prices tumbled another 11 percent over the same period (see Figure 2-1). All told, household and

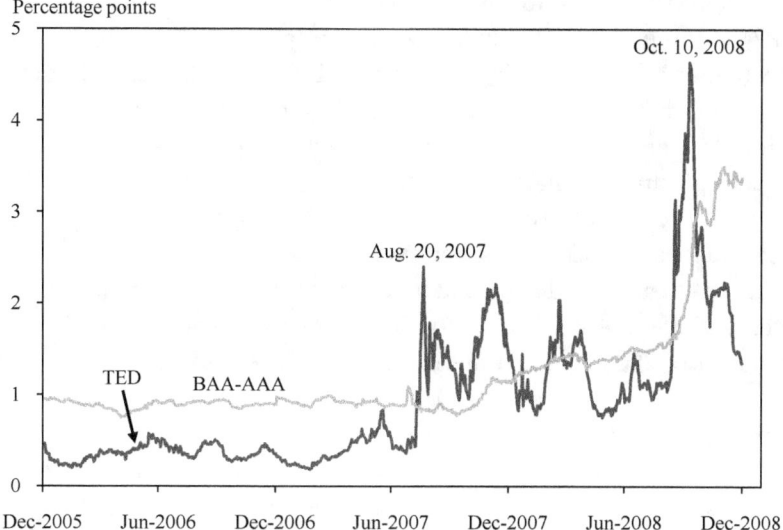

Figure 2-3
TED Spread and Moody's BAA-AAA Spread Through December 2008

Percentage points

Notes: The TED spread is defined as the three-month London Interbank Offered Rate (Libor) less the yield on the three-month U.S. Treasury security. Moody's BAA-AAA spread is the difference between Moody's indexes of yields on AAA and BAA rated corporate bonds.
Source: Bloomberg.

nonprofit net worth declined 20 percent between December 2007 and December 2008, or by about $13 trillion. Again, a useful way to calibrate the size of this shock is to note that in 1929, household wealth declined only 3 percent—about one-seventh as much as in 2008. This is another indication that the shocks hitting the U.S. economy in 2008 were enormous.

The decline in wealth had a severe impact on consumer spending. This key component of aggregate demand, which accounts for roughly 70 percent of GDP and is traditionally quite stable, declined at an annual rate of 3.5 percent in the third quarter of 2008 and 3.1 percent in the fourth quarter. Some of this large decline may have also reflected the surge in uncertainty about future incomes. Not only did asset prices fall sharply, leading to the decline in wealth; they also became dramatically more volatile. The standard deviation of daily stock returns in the fourth quarter, for example, was 4.3 percentage points, even larger than in the first months of the Great Depression.

The financial panic led to a precipitous decline in lending. Bank credit continued to rise over the latter portion of 2008, as households and firms that had lost access to other forms of credit turned to banks. However, bank loans declined sharply in the first and second quarters of 2009 as banks tightened their terms and standards. Other sources of credit showed even more substantial declines. One particularly important market is that for commercial paper (short-term notes issued by firms to finance key operating costs such as payroll and inventory). The market for lower-tier nonfinancial (A2/P2) commercial paper collapsed in the fall of 2008, with the average daily value of new issues falling from $8.0 billion in the second quarter of 2008 to $4.3 billion in the fourth quarter. In addition, securitization of automobile loans, credit card receivables, student loans, and commercial mortgages ground to a halt.

This freezing of credit markets, together with the decline in wealth and confidence, caused consumer spending and residential investment to fall sharply. Real GDP declined at an annual rate of 2.7 percent in the third quarter of 2008, 5.4 percent in the fourth quarter, and 6.4 percent in the first quarter of 2009. Industrial production, which had been falling steadily over the first eight months of 2008, plummeted in the final four months—dropping at an annual rate of 18 percent.

Many industries were battered by the financial crisis and the resulting economic downturn. The American automobile industry was hit particularly hard. Sales of light motor vehicles, which had exceeded 16 million units every year from 1999 to 2007, fell to an annual rate of only 9.5 million in the first quarter of 2009. Employment in the motor vehicle and parts industry declined by 240,000 over the 12 months through January 2009. Two domestic manufacturers, General Motors (GM) and Chrysler, required emergency loans in late December 2008 and early January 2009 to avoid disorderly bankruptcy.

The most disturbing manifestation of the rapid slowdown in the economy was the dramatic increase in job loss. Over the first months of 2008, job losses were typically between 100,000 and 200,000 per month. In October, the economy lost 380,000 jobs; in November, 597,000 jobs. By January, the economy was losing jobs at a rate of 741,000 per month. Commensurate with this terrible rate of job loss, the unemployment rate rose rapidly—from 6.2 percent in September 2008 to 7.7 percent in January 2009. It then continued to rise by roughly one-half of a percentage point per month through the winter and spring; it reached 9.4 percent in May, and ended the year at 10.0 percent.

Wall Street and Main Street

As described in more detail later, policymakers have focused much of their response to the crisis on stabilizing the financial system. Many Americans are troubled by these policies. Because to a large extent it was the actions of credit market participants that led to the crisis, people ask why policymakers should take actions focused on restoring credit markets.

The basic reason for these policies is that the health of credit markets is critically important to the functioning of our economy. Large firms use commercial paper to finance their biweekly payrolls and pay suppliers for materials to keep production lines going. Small firms rely on bank loans to meet their payrolls and pay for supplies while they wait for payment of their accounts receivable. Home purchases depend on mortgages; automobile purchases depend on car loans; college educations depend on student loans; and purchases of everyday items depend on credit cards.

The events of the past two years provide a dramatic demonstration of the importance of credit in the modern economy. As the President said in his inaugural address, "Our workers are no less productive than when this crisis began. Our minds are no less inventive, our goods and services no less needed." Yet developments in financial markets—rises and falls in home and equity prices and in the availability of credit—have led to a collapse of spending, and hence to a precipitous decline in output and to unemployment for millions.

Numerous academic studies before the crisis had also shown that the availability of credit is critical to investment, hiring, and production. One study, for example, found that when a parent company earns high profits and so has less need to rely on credit, the additional funds lead to higher investment by subsidiaries in completely unrelated lines of business (Lamont 1997). Another found that when a small change in a firm's circumstances frees up a large amount of funds that would otherwise have to go to pension contributions, the result is a large change in spending on capital goods (Rauh 2006). Other studies have shown that when the Federal Reserve tightens monetary policy, small firms, which typically have more difficulty obtaining financing, are hit especially hard (Gertler and Gilchrist 1994), and firms without access to public debt markets cut their inventories much more sharply than firms that have such access (Kashyap, Lamont, and Stein 1994).

Research before the crisis had also found that financial market disruptions could affect the real economy. Ben Bernanke, who is now Chairman of the Federal Reserve, demonstrated a link between the disruption of lending caused by bank failures and the worsening of the Great Depression (Bernanke 1983). A smaller but more modern example is provided by the impact of Japan's financial crisis in the 1990s on the United States: construction lending, new construction, and construction employment were more adversely affected in U.S. states where subsidiaries of Japanese banks had a larger role, and thus where credit availability was more affected by the collapse of Japan's bubble (Peek and Rosengren 2000). That a financial disruption in a trading partner can have a detectable adverse impact on our economy through its impact on credit availability suggests that the effect of a full-fledged financial crisis at home would be enormous—an implication that, sadly, has proven to be correct.

Finally, microeconomic evidence from the recent crisis also shows the importance of the financial system to the real economy. For example, firms that happened to have long-term debt coming due after the crisis began, and thus faced high costs of refinancing, cut their investment much more than firms that did not (Almeida et al. 2009). Another study found that a majority of corporate chief financial officers surveyed reported that their firms faced financing constraints during the crisis, and that the constrained firms on average planned to reduce investment spending, research and development, and employment sharply compared with the unconstrained firms (Campello, Graham, and Harvey 2009).

In short, the goal of the policies to stabilize the financial system was not to help financial institutions. The goal was to help ordinary Americans. When the financial system is not working, individuals and businesses cannot get credit, demand and production plummet, and job losses skyrocket. Thus, an essential step in healing the real economy is to heal the financial system. The alternative of letting financial institutions suffer the consequences of their mistakes would have led to a collapse of credit markets and vastly greater suffering for millions and millions of Americans.

The policies to rescue the financial sector were, however, costly, and often had the side effect of benefiting the very institutions whose irresponsible actions contributed to the crisis. That is one reason that the President has endorsed a Financial Crisis Responsibility Fee on the largest financial firms to repay the Federal Government for its extraordinary actions. As discussed in Chapter 6, the Administration has also proposed a comprehensive plan for financial regulatory reform that will help ensure that Wall Street does not return to the risky practices that were a central cause of the recent crisis.

THE UNPRECEDENTED POLICY RESPONSE

Given the magnitude of the shocks that hit the economy in the fall of 2008 and the winter of 2009, the downturn could have turned into a second Great Depression. That it has not is a tribute to the aggressive and effective policy response. This response involved the Federal Reserve and other financial regulators, the Administration, and Congress. The policy tools were similarly multifaceted, including monetary policy, financial market interventions, fiscal policy, and policies targeted specifically at housing.

Monetary Policy

The first line of defense against a weak economy is the interest rate policy of the independent Federal Reserve. By increasing or decreasing the quantity of reserves it supplies to the banking system, the Federal Reserve can lower or raise the Federal funds rate, which is the interest rate at which banks lend to one another. The funds rate influences other interest rates in the economy and so has important effects on economic activity. Using changes in the target level of the funds rate as their main tool of counter-cyclical policy, monetary policymakers had kept inflation low and the real economy remarkably stable for more than two decades.

The Federal Reserve has used interest rate policy aggressively in the recent episode. The target level of the funds rate at the beginning of 2007 was 5¼ percent. The Federal Reserve cut the target by 1 percentage point over the last four months of 2007 and by an additional 2¼ percentage points over the first four months of 2008. After the events of September, it cut the target in three additional steps in October and December, bringing it to its current level of 0 to ¼ percent.

Conventional interest rate policy, however, could do little to deal with the enormous disruptions to credit markets. As a result, the Federal Reserve has used a range of unconventional tools to address those disruptions directly. For example, in March 2008, it created the Primary Dealer Credit Facility and the Term Securities Lending Facility to provide liquidity support for primary dealers (that is, financial institutions that trade directly with the Federal Reserve) and the key financial markets in which they operate. In October 2008, when the critical market for commercial paper threatened to stop functioning, the Federal Reserve responded by setting up the Commercial Paper Funding Facility to backstop the market.

Once the Federal Reserve's target for the funds rate was effectively lowered to zero in December 2008, there was another reason to use unconventional tools. Nominal interest rates generally cannot fall below zero: because holding currency guarantees a nominal return of zero, no one is willing to make loans at a negative nominal interest rate. As a result, when the Federal funds rate is zero, supplying more reserves does not drive it lower. Statistical estimates suggest that based on the Federal Reserve's usual response to inflation and unemployment, the subdued level of inflation and the weak state of the economy would have led the central bank to reduce its target for the funds rate by about an additional 5 percentage points if it could have (Rudebusch 2009).

This desire to provide further stimulus, coupled with the inability to use conventional interest rate policy, led the Federal Reserve to undertake large-scale asset purchases to reduce long-term interest rates. In March

2009, the Federal Reserve announced plans to purchase up to $300 billion of long-term Treasury debt; it also announced plans to increase its purchases of the debt of Fannie Mae, Freddie Mac, and the Federal Home Loan Banks (the government-sponsored enterprises, or GSEs, that support the mortgage market) to up to $200 billion, and its purchases of agency (that is, Fannie Mae, Freddie Mac, and Ginnie Mae) mortgage-backed securities to up to $1.25 trillion.

Finally, the Federal Reserve has attempted to manage expectations by providing information about its goals and the likely path of policy. Officials have consistently stressed their commitment to ensuring that inflation neither falls substantially below nor rises substantially above its usual level. In addition, the Federal Reserve has repeatedly stated that economic conditions "are likely to warrant exceptionally low levels of the Federal funds rate for an extended period." To the extent this statement provides market participants with information they did not already have, it is likely to keep longer-term interest rates lower than they otherwise would be.

One effect of the Federal Reserve's unconventional policies has been an enormous expansion of the quantity of assets on the Federal Reserve's balance sheet. Figure 2-4 shows the evolution of Federal Reserve asset holdings since the beginning of 2007. One can see both that asset holdings nearly tripled between January and December 2008 and that there was a dramatic move away from short-term Treasury securities.

Figure 2-4
Assets on the Federal Reserve's Balance Sheet

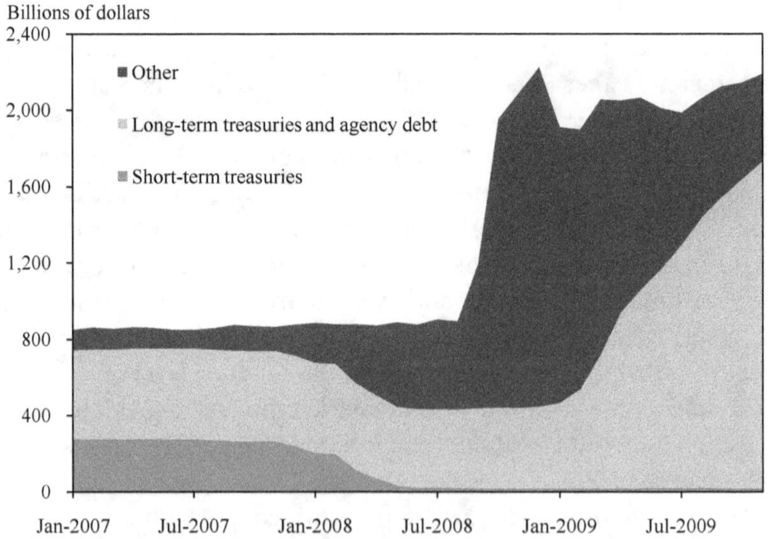

Notes: Agency debt refers to obligations of Fannie Mae, Freddie Mac, and the Federal Home Loan Banks. Agency mortgage-backed securities are also included in this category.
Source: Federal Reserve Board, H.4.1 Table 1.

The flip side of the large increase in the Federal Reserve's asset holdings is a large increase in the quantity of reserves it has supplied to the financial system. Some observers have expressed concern that the large expansion in reserves could lead to inflation. In this regard, two key points should be kept in mind. First, as already described, most statistical models suggest that the Federal Reserve's target interest rate would be substantially lower than it is today if it were not constrained by the fact that the Federal funds rate cannot fall below zero. As a result, monetary policy is in fact unusually tight given the state of the economy, not unusually loose. Second, the Federal Reserve has the tools it needs to prevent the reserves from leading to inflation. It can drain the reserves from the financial system through sales of the assets it has acquired or other actions. Indeed, despite the weak state of the economy, the return of credit market conditions toward normal is leading to the natural unwinding of some of the exceptional credit market programs. Another reliable way the Federal Reserve can keep the reserves from creating inflationary pressure is by using its relatively new ability to raise the interest rate it pays on reserves: banks will be unwilling to lend the reserves at low interest rates if they can obtain a higher return on their balances held at the Federal Reserve.

Financial Rescue

Efforts to stabilize the financial system have been a central part of the policy response. As just discussed, even before the financial crisis in September 2008, the Federal Reserve was taking steps to ease pressures on credit markets. The events of the fall led to even stronger actions. On September 7, Fannie Mae and Freddie Mac were placed in conservatorship under the Federal Housing Finance Agency to prevent a potentially severe disruption of mortgage lending. On September 16, concern about the potentially catastrophic effects of a disorderly failure of American International Group (AIG) caused the Federal Reserve to extend the firm an $85 billion line of credit. On September 19, concerns about the possibility of runs on money-market mutual funds led the Treasury to announce a temporary guarantee program for these funds.

On October 3, Congress passed and President Bush signed the Emergency Economic Stabilization Act of 2008. This Act provided up to $700 billion for the Troubled Asset Relief Program (TARP) for the purchase of distressed assets and for capital injections into financial institutions, although the second $350 billion required presidential notification to Congress and could be disallowed by a vote of both houses. The initial $350 billion was used mainly to purchase preferred equity shares in financial institutions, thereby providing the institutions with more capital to help them withstand the crisis.

At President-Elect Obama's request, President Bush notified Congress on January 12, 2009 of his plan to release the second $350 billion of TARP funds. With strong support from the incoming Administration, the Senate defeated a resolution disapproving the release. These funds provided policy-makers with critical resources needed to ensure financial stability.

On February 10, 2009, Secretary of the Treasury Timothy Geithner announced the Administration's Financial Stability Plan. The plan represented a new, comprehensive approach to the financial rescue that sought to tackle the interlocking sources of instability and increase credit flows. An overarching theme was a focus on transparency and accountability to rebuild confidence in financial markets and protect taxpayer resources.

A key element of the plan was the Supervisory Capital Assessment Program (or "stress test"). The purpose was to assess the capital needs of the country's 19 largest financial institutions should economic and financial conditions deteriorate further. Institutions that were found to need an additional capital buffer would be encouraged to raise private capital and would be provided with temporary government capital if those efforts did not succeed. This program was intended not just to examine the capital positions of the institutions and ensure that they obtained more capital if needed, but also to strengthen private investors' confidence in the soundness of the institutions' balance sheets, and so strengthen the institutions' ability to obtain private capital.

Another element of the plan was the Consumer and Business Lending Initiative, which was aimed at maintaining the flow of credit. In November 2008, the Federal Reserve had created the Term Asset-Backed Securities Loan Facility to help counteract the dramatic decline in securitized lending. In the February announcement of the Financial Stability Plan, the Treasury greatly expanded the resources of the not-yet-implemented facility. The Treasury increased its commitment to $100 billion to leverage up to $1 trillion of lending for businesses and households. By facilitating securitization, the program was designed to help unfreeze credit and lower interest rates for auto loans, credit card loans, student loans, and small business loans guaranteed by the Small Business Administration (SBA).

A third element of the plan was a Treasury partnership with the Federal Deposit Insurance Corporation and the Federal Reserve to create the Public-Private Investment Program. A central purpose was to remove troubled assets from the balance sheets of financial institutions, thereby reducing uncertainty about their financial strength and increasing their ability to raise capital and hence their willingness to lend. Partnership with the private sector served two important objectives: it leveraged scarce public funds, and it used private competition and incentives to ensure that the government did not overpay for assets.

There were two other key components of the Financial Stability Plan. One was a wide-ranging program to reduce mortgage interest rates and help responsible homeowners stay in their homes. These policies are described later in the section on housing policy. The other component was a range of measures to help small businesses. Many of these were included in the American Recovery and Reinvestment Act and are discussed in the section on fiscal stimulus.

Failure of the two troubled domestic automakers (GM and Chrysler) threatened economy-wide repercussions that would have been magnified by related problems at the automakers' associated financial institutions (GMAC and Chrysler Financial). To avoid these consequences, the Bush Administration set up the Auto Industry Financing Program within the TARP. This program extended $17.4 billion in funding to the two companies in late December 2008 and early January 2009. The program also extended $7.5 billion in funding to the two auto finance companies around the same time. Upon taking office, the Obama Administration required the automakers to submit plans for restructuring and a return to viability before additional funds were committed. To sustain the industry during this planning process, the Treasury established the Warranty Commitment Program to reassure consumers that warranties of the troubled firms would be honored. It also initiated the Auto Supplier Support Program to maintain stability in the auto supply base.

Over the spring of 2009, the Administration's Auto Task Force worked with GM and Chrysler to produce plans for viability. In the case of Chrysler, the task force determined that viability could be achieved by merging with the Italian automaker Fiat. For GM, the task force determined that substantial reductions in costs were necessary and charged the company with producing a more aggressive restructuring plan. For both companies, a quick, targeted bankruptcy was judged to be the most efficient and successful way to restructure. Chrysler filed for bankruptcy on April 30, 2009; GM, on June 1. In addition to concessions by all stakeholders, including workers, retirees, creditors, and suppliers, the U.S. Government invested substantial funds to bring about the orderly restructuring. In all, more than $80 billion of TARP funds had been authorized for the motor vehicle industry as of September 20, 2009.

Fiscal Stimulus

The signature element of the Administration's policy response to the crisis was the American Recovery and Reinvestment Act of 2009 (ARRA). The President signed the Recovery Act in Denver on February 17, just 28 days after taking office. At an estimated cost of $787 billion, the Act is the largest countercyclical fiscal action in American history. It provides tax cuts and increases in government spending equivalent to roughly 2 percent of GDP in 2009 and 2¼ percent of GDP in 2010. To put those figures in perspective, the largest expansionary swing in the budget during Franklin Roosevelt's New Deal was an increase in the deficit of about 1½ percent of GDP in fiscal 1936. That expansion, however, was counteracted the very next fiscal year by a contraction that was even larger.

The fiscal stimulus was designed to fill part of the shortfall in aggregate demand caused by the collapse of private demand and the Federal Reserve's inability to lower short-term interest rates further. It was part of a comprehensive package that included stabilizing the financial system, helping responsible homeowners avoid foreclosure, and aiding small businesses through tax relief and increased lending. The President set as a goal for the fiscal stimulus that it raise employment by 3½ million relative to what it otherwise would have been.

Several principles guided the design of the stimulus. One was that it be spread over two years, reflecting the Administration's view that the economy would need substantial support for more than one year. At the same time, the Administration also strongly supported keeping the stimulus explicitly temporary. It was not to be an excuse to permanently expand the size of government.

A second key principle was that the stimulus be well diversified. Different types of stimulus affect the economy in different ways. Individual tax cuts, for example, affect production and employment in a wide range of industries by encouraging households to spend more on consumer goods, while government investments in infrastructure directly increase construction activity and employment. In addition, underlying economic conditions affect the efficacy of fiscal policy in ways that can be quantitatively important and sometimes difficult to forecast. Likewise, different types of stimulus affect the economy with different speeds. For instance, aid to individuals directly affected by the recession tends to be spent relatively quickly, while new investment projects require more time. Because of the need to provide broad support to the economy over an extended period, the Administration supported a stimulus plan that included a broad range of fiscal actions.

A third principle was that emergency spending should aim to address long-term needs. Some spending, such as unemployment insurance, is aimed at helping those directly affected by the recession maintain a decent standard of living. But government investment spending should aim to create enduring capital investments that increase productivity and growth.

The Recovery Act reflected those guiding principles. The Congressional Budget Office (CBO) estimated that almost one-quarter of the stimulus would be spent by the end of the third quarter of 2009, and an additional half would be spent over the next four quarters (Congressional Budget Office 2009b). So far, the pace of the spending and tax cuts has largely matched CBO's estimates.

The final package was very well diversified. Roughly one-third took the form of tax cuts. The most significant of these was the Making Work Pay tax credit, which cut taxes for 95 percent of working families. Taxes for a typical family were reduced by $800 per couple for each of 2009 and 2010. Another provision of the bill provided roughly $14 billion for one-time payments of $250 to seniors, veterans, and people with disabilities. The macroeconomic effects of these payments are likely to be similar to those of tax cuts.

Businesses received important tax cuts as well. The most important of these was an extension of bonus depreciation, which reduced taxes on new investments by allowing firms to immediately deduct half the cost of property and equipment purchases. One advantage of such temporary investment incentives is that they can affect the timing of investment, moving some investment from future years when the economy does not have a deficiency of aggregate demand to the present, when it does.

In addition, because the financial market disruptions had a particularly paralyzing effect on the financial plans of small businesses, the Act included additional measures targeted specifically at those businesses. Tax cuts for small businesses included an expansion of provisions allowing for the carryback of net operating losses, a temporary 75 percent exclusion from capital gains taxes on small business stock, and the ability to immediately expense up to $250,000 of qualified investment purchases. In addition to reducing taxes, these provisions improve cash flow at firms facing credit constraints and provide extra incentives for individuals to invest in small businesses. The Act also included measures to help increase small business lending through the SBA. In particular, it raised to 90 percent the maximum guarantee on SBA general purpose and working capital loans (the 7(a) program) and eliminated fees on both 7(a) loans and loans for fixed-asset capital and real estate investment projects (the 504 program).

Another important part of the stimulus consisted of fiscal relief to state governments. Because almost every state has a balanced-budget requirement, the declines in revenues caused by the recession forced states to cut spending or raise taxes, thereby further contracting demand and magnifying the downturn. Federal fiscal relief can help prevent these contractionary responses, helping to maintain critical state services and state employment, prevent tax increases on families already suffering from the recession, and cushion the fall in demand. And because many states were already raising taxes and cutting spending when the ARRA was passed, the effects were likely to occur relatively quickly. The Act therefore included roughly $140 billion of state fiscal relief.

The Recovery Act also included approximately $90 billion of support for individuals directly affected by the recession. This support serves two critical purposes. First, it provides relief from the recession's devastating impact on families and individuals. Second, because the recipients typically spend this support quickly, it provides an immediate boost to the broader economy. Among the major components of this relief were an extension and expansion of unemployment insurance benefits, subsidies to help the unemployed continue to obtain health insurance, and additional funding for the Supplemental Nutritional Assistance Program. The Act also reduced taxes on unemployment insurance benefits, the effect of which is similar to an expansion of benefits.

Finally, the Recovery Act included direct government investment spending. Because government investment raises output in the short run both through its direct effects and by increasing the incomes and spending of the workers employed on the projects, its output effects are particularly large. In addition, because this type of stimulus is spent less quickly than other types, it will play a vital role in providing support to the economy after 2009. And by funding critical investments, this spending will raise the economy's output even in the long run.

The Act included funding both for traditional government investment projects, such as transportation infrastructure and basic scientific research, and for initial investments to jump-start private investment in emerging new areas, such as health information technology, a smart electrical grid, and clean energy technologies. The Act also included tax credits for specific types of private spending, such as home weatherization and advanced energy manufacturing, which are likely to have effects similar to direct government investment spending. Altogether, roughly one-third of the budget impact of the Recovery Act will take the form of these investments and tax credits.

Fiscal stimulus actions did not end with the passage and implementation of the Recovery Act. In June 2009, the Administration worked with Congress to set up the Car Allowance Rebate System (CARS). Commonly known as the "Cash for Clunkers" program, CARS gave rebates of up to $4,500 to consumers who replaced older cars and trucks with newer, more fuel-efficient models. The program was in effect for July and most of August. After the program's popularity led to quick exhaustion of the original funding of $1 billion, the funding was increased to $3 billion to allow more consumers to participate.

In November, the Worker, Homeownership, and Business Assistance Act of 2009 cut taxes for struggling businesses and strengthened the safety net for workers. In particular, the Act extended the net operating loss provisions of the Recovery Act that allowed small businesses to count their losses this year against taxes paid in previous years for an additional year, and expanded the benefit to medium and large businesses. The Act also provided up to 20 additional weeks of unemployment insurance benefits for workers who were reaching the end of their emergency unemployment benefits. In December, an amendment to the Department of Defense Appropriations Act of 2010 continued through the end of February 2010 the unemployment insurance provisions of the Recovery Act, the November extension of emergency benefits, and the COBRA subsidy program that helps unemployed workers maintain their health insurance. It also expanded the COBRA premium subsidy period from 9 to 15 months and extended the increased guarantees and fee waivers for SBA loans.

Housing Policy

The economic and financial crisis began in the housing market, and an important part of the policy response has been directed at that market. The Administration initiated the Making Home Affordable program (MHA) in March 2009. This program was designed to support low mortgage rates, keep millions of homeowners in their homes, and stabilize the housing market.

As described earlier, the Federal Reserve undertook large-scale purchases of GSE debt and mortgage-backed securities in an effort to reduce mortgage interest rates. At the same time, the Treasury Department made an increased funding commitment to the GSEs. This increased government support for the agencies also reduced their borrowing costs and so helped lower mortgage interest rates.

Importantly, MHA also included a program to help households take advantage of lower interest rates. The Home Affordable Refinance Program helps families whose homes have lost value and whose mortgage payments can be reduced by refinancing at historically low interest rates. This program expanded the opportunity to refinance to borrowers with loans owned or guaranteed by the GSEs who had a mortgage balance up to 125 percent of their home's current value.

Another key component of MHA is the Home Affordable Modification Program (HAMP), which is providing up to $75 billion to encourage loan modifications. It offers incentives to investors, lenders, servicers, and homeowners to encourage mortgage modifications in which all stakeholders share in the cost of ensuring that responsible homeowners can afford their monthly mortgage payments. To protect taxpayers, HAMP focuses on sound modifications. No payments are made by the government unless the modification lasts for at least three months, and all the payments are designed around the principle of "pay for success." All parties have aligned incentives under the program to achieve successful modifications at an affordable and sustainable level.

The Administration has supported additional programs to help the housing sector. The Recovery Act included an $8,000 first-time homebuyer's credit for home purchases made before December 1, 2009. As with temporary investment incentives, this credit can help the economy by changing the timing of decisions, bringing buyers into the housing market who were not planning on becoming homeowners until after 2009 or were postponing their purchases in light of the distress in the market. In November, this credit was expanded and extended by the Workers, Homeownership, and Business Assistance Act of 2009.

The Recovery Act also gave considerable resources to the Neighborhood Stabilization Program, a program administered by the Department of Housing and Urban Development to stabilize communities that have suffered from foreclosures and abandoned homes. The Administration also provided assistance to state and local housing finance agencies and their efforts to aid distressed homeowners, stimulate first-time home buying, and provide affordable rental homes. These agencies had faced a significant liquidity crisis resulting from disruptions in financial markets.

THE EFFECTS OF THE POLICIES

The condition of the American economy has changed dramatically in the past year. At the beginning of 2009, financial markets were functioning poorly, house prices were plummeting, and output and employment were in freefall. Today, financial markets have stabilized and credit is starting to flow again, house prices have leveled off, output is growing, and the employment situation is stabilizing. Because of the depth of the economy's fall, we are a long way from full recovery, and significant challenges remain. But the trajectory of the economy is vastly improved.

There is strong evidence that the policy response has been central to this turnaround. The actions to stabilize credit markets have prevented further destructive failures of major financial institutions and helped maintain lending in key areas. The housing and mortgage policies have kept hundreds of thousands of homeowners in their homes and brought mortgage rates to historic lows. The speed of the economy's change in direction has been remarkable and matches up well with the timing of the fiscal stimulus. And both direct estimates as well as the assessments of expert observers underscore the crucial role played by the stimulus.

The Financial Sector

Given the powerful impact of the financial sector on the real economy, a necessary first step to recovery of the real economy was recovery of the financial sector. And the financial sector has unquestionably begun to recover. Figure 2-5 extends the graph of the TED spread and the BAA-AAA spread shown in Figure 2-3 through December 2009. After spiking to unprecedented levels in October 2008, the TED spread fell rapidly over the next two months but remained substantially elevated at the beginning of 2009. It then declined gradually through August and is now at normal levels. This key indicator of the basic functioning of credit markets suggests substantial financial recovery. The BAA-AAA spread remained very high through April but then fell rapidly from April to September. This spread, which normally rises when the economy is weak because of higher corporate default risks, is now at levels comparable to those at the beginning of the recession and below its levels in much of 1990–91 and 2002–03. Thus, the current level of the spread appears to reflect mainly the weak state of the economy rather than any specific difficulties in credit markets.

Figure 2-5
TED Spread and Moody's BAA-AAA Spread Through December 2009

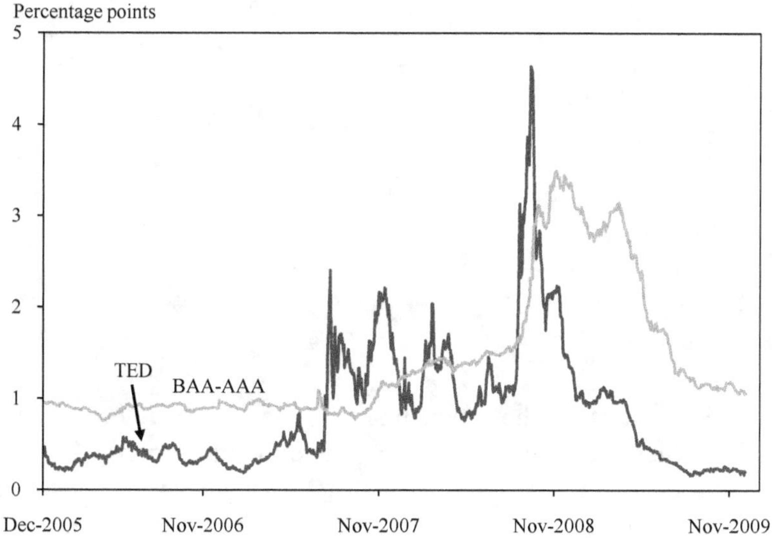

Percentage points

Notes: The TED spread is defined as the three-month London Interbank Offer Rate (LIBOR) less the yield on the three-month U.S. Treasury security. Moody's BAA-AAA spread is the difference between Moody's indexes of yields on AAA and BAA rated corporate bonds.
Source: Bloomberg.

Another broad indicator of the health of the financial system is the level of stock prices, which depend both on investors' expectations of future earnings and on their willingness to bear risk. Figure 2-6 shows the behavior of the S&P 500 stock price index since January 2006. This series declined by 18 percent from its peak in October 2007 through the end of August 2008, fell precipitously in September, and continued to fall through March 2009 as the economy deteriorated sharply and investors became extremely fearful. The stabilization of the economy and the restoration of more normal workings of financial markets have led to a sharp turnaround in stock prices. As of December 31, 2009, the S&P 500 was 65 percent above its low in March. As with the BAA-AAA spread, the current level of stock prices relative to their pre-recession level appears to reflect the weaker situation of the real economy rather than any specific problems with financial markets or investors' willingness to bear risk.

Figure 2-6
S&P 500 Stock Price Index

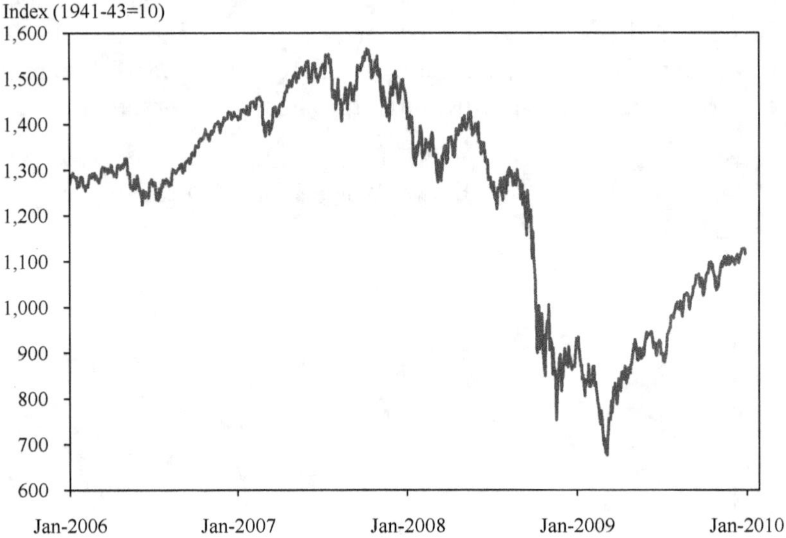

Source: Bloomberg.

These indicators show that financial markets have evolved toward normalcy, which was a necessary step in stopping the economic freefall. But for the economy to recover fully, that is not enough: credit must be available to sound borrowers. On this front, the results are more mixed. Some sources of credit are coming back strongly, but others remain weak.

As described in more detail later, one critical market where policies have succeeded in lowering interest rates and maintaining credit flows is the mortgage market. Another market that has recovered substantially is the market for commercial paper. In late 2008 and early 2009, this market was functioning in large part because of the direct intervention of the Federal Reserve. By mid-January, the Federal Reserve's Commercial Paper Funding Facility (CPFF) was holding $350 billion of commercial paper. As credit conditions have stabilized, however, firms have been able to place their commercial paper privately on better terms than through the CPFF, and levels of commercial paper outstanding have remained stable even as the Federal Reserve has reduced its holdings to less than $15 billion. Nonetheless, quantities of commercial paper outstanding remain well below their pre-crisis levels.

Another crucial source of credit that has stabilized is the market for corporate bonds. As risk spreads have fallen, corporations have found it easier to obtain funding by issuing longer-term bonds than by issuing such instruments as commercial paper. As a result, corporate bond issuance, which fell sharply in the second half of 2008, is now running above pre-crisis levels.

An important financial market development occurred in response to the stress test conducted in the spring. This comprehensive review of the soundness of the Nation's 19 largest financial institutions, together with the public release of this information, strengthened private investors' confidence in the institutions. Partly as a result, the institutions were able to raise $55 billion in private common equity, improving their capital positions and their ability to lend.

The fact that financial institutions are increasingly able to raise private capital is reducing their need to rely on public capital. Only $7 billion of TARP funds have been extended to banks since January 20, 2009. Many financial institutions have repaid their TARP funds, and the expected cost of the program to the government has been revised down by approximately $200 billion since August 2009.

Policy initiatives have also had a clear impact on small business lending. Figure 2-7 shows the amount of SBA-guaranteed loans that have been made since October 2006. SBA loan volume experienced its first significant decrease in September and October 2007; following the failure of Lehman Brothers in September 2008, it fell by more than half. The recovery in small business lending coincided with the passage of the Recovery Act in February 2009. In the months between Lehman's fall and passage of the Recovery Act, average monthly loan volume was $830 million; immediately after passage, loan volume began to steadily recover and averaged $1.3 billion per month through September 2009. In September, loan volume reached $1.9 billion, which was the highest level since August 2007; this has since been exceeded by November 2009's monthly loan volume of

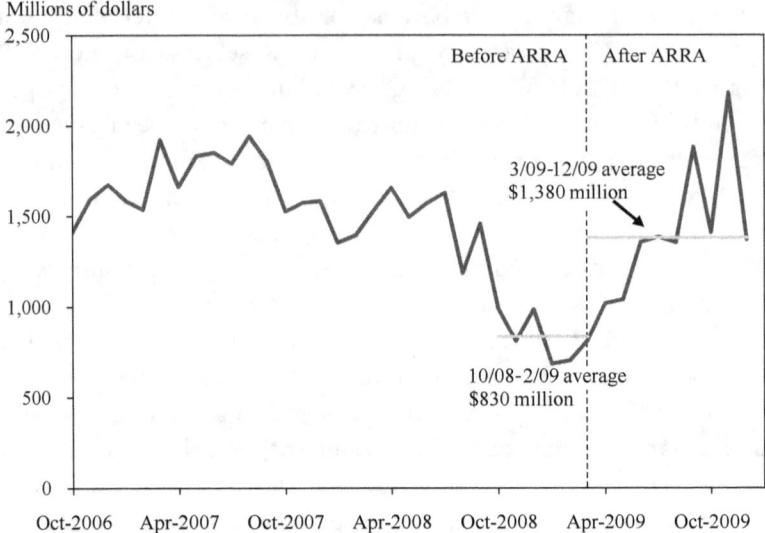

Figure 2-7
Monthly Gross SBA 7(a) and 504 Loan Approvals

Millions of dollars

Before ARRA | After ARRA

3/09-12/09 average
$1,380 million

10/08-2/09 average
$830 million

Oct-2006   Apr-2007   Oct-2007   Apr-2008   Oct-2008   Apr-2009   Oct-2009

Source: Unpublished monthly data provided by the Small Business Administration.

$2.2 billion. In total, between February and December 2009 the SBA guaranteed nearly $15 billion in small business lending.

Nonetheless, overall credit conditions have not returned to normal. Many small business owners report continued difficulties in obtaining credit. In addition, the severity of the downturn is leading to elevated rates of failure of small banks, potentially disrupting their lending to small businesses and households. The market for asset-backed securities is also far from fully recovered. As a result, it is often hard for banks and other lenders to package and sell their loans, which forces them to hold a greater fraction of the loans they originate and thus limits their ability to lend.

One important source of data on credit availability is the Federal Reserve's Senior Loan Officer Opinion Survey on Bank Lending Practices. The survey, conducted every three months, examines whether banks are tightening lending standards, loosening them, or keeping them basically unchanged. The October 2008 survey found that the overwhelming majority of banks were tightening standards. This fraction has declined steadily, and by October 2009 less than 20 percent were reporting that they were tightening standards for commercial and industrial loans, though none reported loosening standards. Thus, credit conditions remain tight.

Housing

As described earlier, policymakers have taken unprecedented actions to maintain mortgage lending. One result has been a major shift in the composition of mortgage finance. In 2006, private institutions provided 60 percent of liquidity while the GSEs, the Federal Housing Agency (FHA), and the Veterans Administration (VA) provided the remaining 40 percent. As home prices began to decline nationally in 2007, private financing for mortgages began to dry up. As of November 2009, the mortgages guaranteed by the GSEs, FHA, and the VA accounted for nearly all mortgage originations. About 22 percent of mortgage originations are guaranteed by FHA or VA, up from less than 3 percent in 2006. About 75 percent of mortgage originations are guaranteed by the GSEs, up from less than 40 percent in 2006.

As Figure 2-8 shows, mortgage rates fell to historic lows in 2009— consistent with the government's increased funding commitment to Fannie Mae and Freddie Mac and the Federal Reserve's purchases of mortgage-backed securities. These low mortgage rates support home prices and thus benefit all homeowners. More directly, households that have refinanced their mortgages at the lower rates have obtained considerable savings. These savings have effects similar to tax cuts, improving households' financial positions and encouraging spending on other goods. With the help of the Home Affordable Refinance Program, approximately 3 million borrowers have refinanced, putting more than $6 billion of purchasing power at an annual rate into the hands of households.

Figure 2-8
30-Year Fixed Rate Mortgage Rate

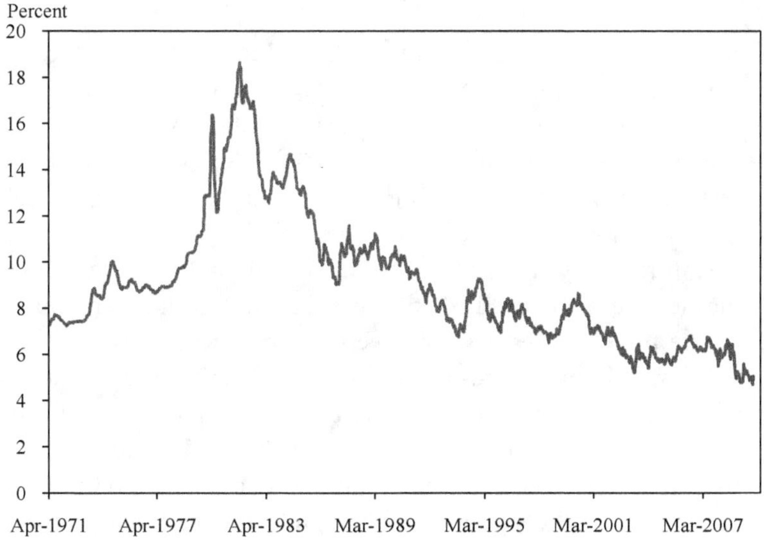

Note: Contract interest rate for first mortgages.
Source: Freddie Mac, Primary Mortgage Market Survey.

In addition, the Home Affordable Modification Program has been successful in encouraging mortgage modifications. When the program was launched, the Administration estimated that it could offer help to as many as 3 million to 4 million borrowers through the end of 2012. On October 8, 2009, the Administration announced that servicers had begun more than 500,000 trial modifications, nearly a month ahead of the original goal. As of November, the monthly pace of trial modifications exceeded the monthly pace of completed foreclosures. Of course, not all trial modifications will become permanent, but the Administration is making every effort to ensure that as many sound modifications as possible do.

One important result of the policies aimed at the housing market and of the broader policies to support the economy is that the housing market appears to have stabilized. National home price indexes have been relatively steady for the past several months, as shown in Figure 2-9. The Federal Housing Finance Agency purchase-only house price index, which is constructed using only conforming mortgages (that is, mortgages eligible for purchase by the GSEs), has changed little since late 2008. The LoanPerformance house price index, another closely watched measure that uses conforming and nonconforming mortgages with coverage of repeat sales transactions for more than 85 percent of the population, rose 6 percent between March and August 2009 before declining slightly in recent months. In addition, the pace of sales of existing single-family homes has increased substantially. Sales in the fourth quarter of 2009 were 29 percent above their low in the first quarter of 2009 and comparable to levels in the first half of 2007.

Finally, there are signs of renewed building activity. After falling 81 percent from their peak in September 2005 to their low in January 2009, single-family housing permits (a leading indicator of housing construction) rose 49 percent through December 2009. Similarly, after falling for 14 consecutive quarters, the residential investment component of real GDP rose in the third and fourth quarters of 2009.

Inventories of vacant homes for sale remain at high levels, and many vacant homes are being held off the market and will likely be put up for sale as home prices increase. This overhang may lead to some additional price declines, although prices are unlikely to fall at the same rate as they did during the crisis. Thus, the recovery of the housing sector is likely to be slow. Of course, we should neither expect nor want the housing market to return to its pre-crisis condition. In the long run, as discussed in more detail in Chapter 4, neither the extraordinarily high levels of housing construction and price appreciation before the crisis nor the extraordinarily low levels of construction and the rapid price declines during the crisis are sustainable.

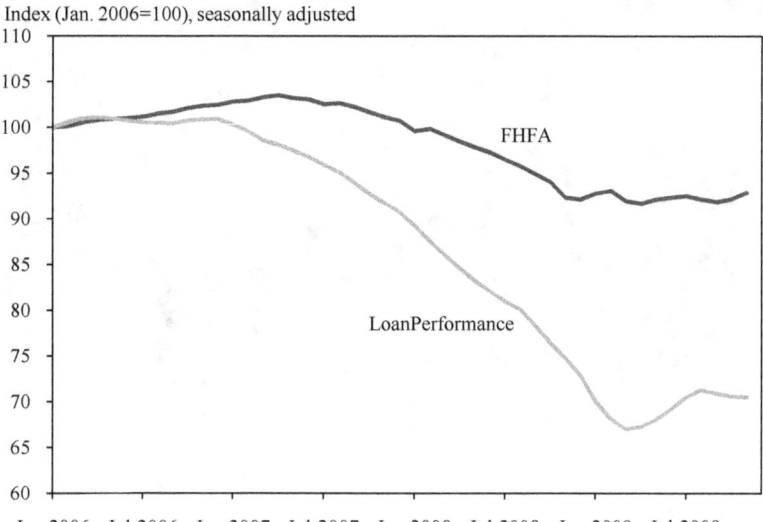

Figure 2-9
FHFA and LoanPerformance National House Price Indexes

Index (Jan. 2006=100), seasonally adjusted

FHFA

LoanPerformance

Sources: Federal Housing Finance Agency, purchase-only index; First American Core Logic LoanPerformance.

Overall Economic Activity

The direction of overall economic activity changed dramatically over the course of 2009. Figure 2-10 shows the quarterly growth rate of real GDP, the broadest indicator of national production. After falling at an annual rate of 6.4 percent in the first quarter, real GDP declined at a rate of just 0.7 percent in the second quarter. It then grew at a 2.2 percent rate in the third quarter and a 5.7 percent rate in the fourth. Such a rapid turnaround in growth is remarkable. The improvement in growth of 8.6 percentage points from the first quarter to the third quarter (that is, the swing from growth at a -6.4 percent rate to growth at a 2.2 percent rate) was the largest since 1983. Similarly, the three-quarter improvement from the first quarter to the fourth of 12.1 percentage points was the largest since 1981, and the second largest since 1958.

One limitation of these simple statistics is that they do not account for the usual dynamics of the economy. A more sophisticated way to gauge the extent of the change in the economy's direction is to compare the path the economy has followed with the predictions of a statistical model. There are many ways to construct a baseline statistical forecast. The particular one used here is a vector autoregression (or VAR) that includes the logarithms of real GDP (in billions of chained 2005 dollars) and payroll employment (in thousands, in the final month of the quarter), using four lags of each variable

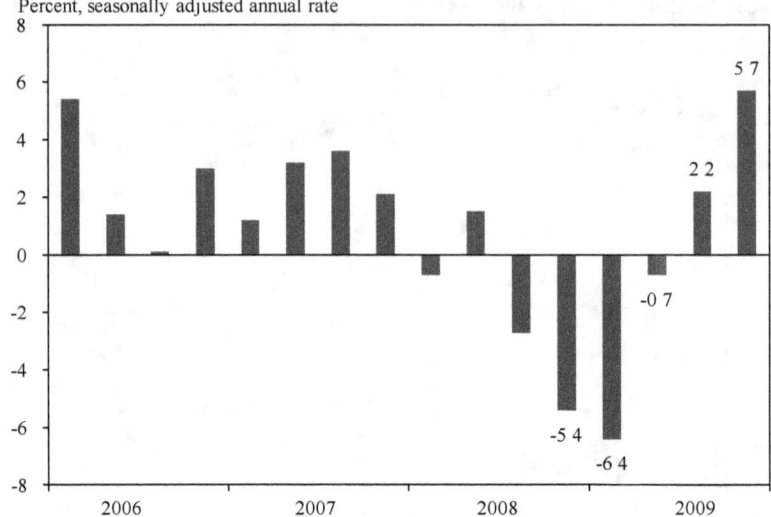

Figure 2-10
Real GDP Growth

Percent, seasonally adjusted annual rate

Source: Department of Commerce (Bureau of Economic Analysis), National Income and
Product Accounts Table 1.1.1, line 1.

and estimated over the period 1990:Q1–2007:Q4. Because the sample period
ends in the fourth quarter of 2007, the coefficient estimates used to construct
the forecast are not influenced by the current recession. Rather, they show
the normal joint short-run dynamics of real GDP and employment over an
extended period. GDP and employment are then forecast for the final three
quarters of 2009 using the estimated VAR and actual data through the first
quarter of the year. The resulting comparison of the actual and projected
paths of the economy shows the differences between the economy's actual
performance and what one would have expected given the situation as of
the first quarter and the economy's usual dynamics.[1] Although the results
presented here are based on one specific approach to constructing the
baseline projection, other reasonable approaches have similar implications.

This more sophisticated exercise also finds that the economy's
turnaround has been impressive. The statistical forecast based on the economy's normal dynamics projects growth at a -3.3 percent rate in the second
quarter of 2009, -0.5 percent in the third, and 1.3 percent in the fourth. In
all three quarters, actual growth was substantially higher than the projection.
Figure 2-11 shows that as a result, the *level* of GDP exceeded the projected
level by an increasing margin: 0.7 percent in the second quarter, 1.4 percent
in the third quarter, and 2.5 percent in the fourth.

---

[1] For more details on this approach and the model-based approach discussed later, see Council
of Economic Advisers (2010).

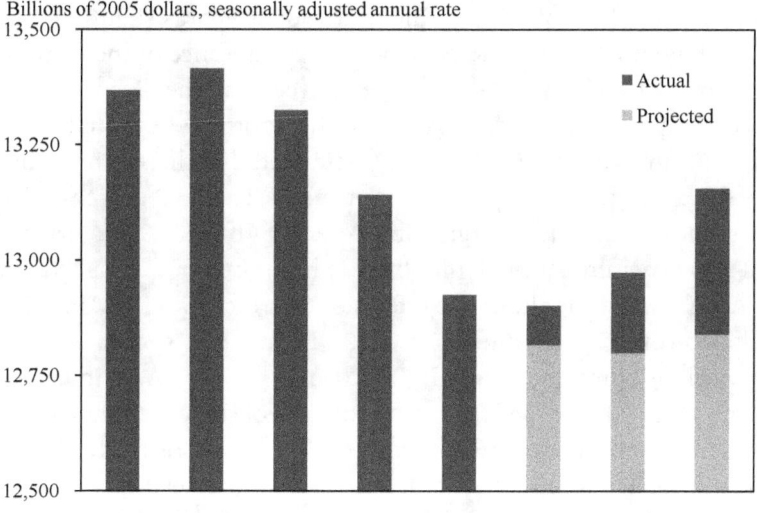

Figure 2-11
Real GDP: Actual and Statistical Baseline Projection

Billions of 2005 dollars, seasonally adjusted annual rate

Sources: Department of Commerce (Bureau of Economic Analysis), National Income and Product Accounts Table 1.1.6, line 1; CEA calculations. See Council of Economic Advisers (2010).

The gap between the actual and projected paths of GDP provides a rough way to estimate the effect of economic policy. The most obvious sources of the differences are the unprecedented policy actions. However, the gap reflects all unusual influences on GDP. For example, the rescue actions taken in other countries (described in Chapter 3) could have played a role in better American performance. At the same time, the continuing stringency in credit markets is likely lowering output relative to its usual cyclical patterns. Thus, while some factors work in the direction of causing the comparison of the economy's actual performance with its normal behavior to overstate the contribution of economic policy actions, others work in the opposite direction.

One way to estimate the specific impact of the Recovery Act is to use estimates from economic models. Mainstream estimates of economic multipliers for the effects of fiscal policy can be combined with figures on the stimulus to date to estimate how much the stimulus has contributed to growth. (For the financial and housing policies, this approach is not feasible, because the policies are so unprecedented that no estimates of their effects are readily available.) When this exercise is performed using the multipliers employed by the Council of Economic Advisers (CEA), which are based on mainstream economic models, the results suggest a critical role for the fiscal stimulus. They suggest that the Recovery Act contributed approximately 2.8

percentage points to *growth* in the second quarter, 3.9 percentage points in the third, and 1.8 percentage points in the fourth. As a result, this approach suggests that the *level* of GDP in the fourth quarter was slightly more than 2 percent higher than it would have been in the absence of the stimulus.

Knowledgeable outside observers agree that the Recovery Act has increased output substantially relative to what it otherwise would have been. For example, in November 2009, CBO estimated that the Act had raised the level of output in the third quarter by between 1.2 and 3.2 percent relative to the no-stimulus baseline (Congressional Budget Office 2009a). Private forecasters also generally estimate that the Act has raised output substantially.

A final way to look for the effects of the rescue policies on GDP is in the behavior of the components of GDP. Figure 2-12 shows the contribution of various components of GDP to overall GDP growth in each of the four quarters of 2009. One area where policy's role seems clear is in business investment in equipment and software. A key source of the turnaround in GDP is the change in this type of investment from a devastating 36 percent annual rate of decline in the first quarter to a 13 percent rate of increase by the fourth quarter. Two likely contributors to this change were the investment incentives in the Recovery Act and the many measures to stabilize the financial system and maintain lending. Similarly, the housing and financial

Figure 2-12
Contributions to Real GDP Growth

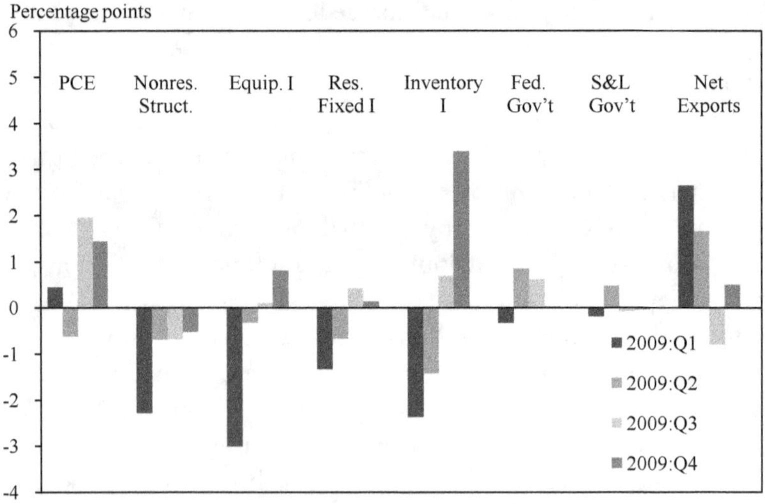

Notes: Bars sum to quarterly change in GDP growth (-6.4% in Q1; -0.7% in Q2; 2 2% in Q3; 5.7% in Q4). PCE is personal consumption expenditures; Nonres. Struct. is nonresidential fixed investment in structures; Equip I. is nonresidential fixed investment in equipment and software; Res. Fixed I is residential fixed investment; Inventory I is inventory investment; Federal Gov't is Federal Government purchases; S&L Gov't is state and local government purchases; Net Exports is net exports.
Source: Department of Commerce (Bureau of Economic Analysis), National Income and Product Accounts Table 1.1.2.

market policies were surely important to the swing in the growth of residential investment from a 38 percent annual rate of decline in the first quarter to increases in the third and fourth quarters.

Two other components showing evidence of the policies' effects are personal consumption expenditures and state and local government purchases. The Making Work Pay tax credit and the aid to individuals directly affected by the recession meant that households did not have to cut their consumption spending as much as they otherwise would have, and the Cash for Clunkers program provided important incentives for motor vehicle purchases in the third quarter. Consumption was little changed in the first two quarters of 2009 and then rose at a healthy 2.8 percent annual rate in the third quarter—driven in considerable part by a 44 percent rate of increase in purchases of motor vehicles and parts—and at a 2.0 percent rate in the fourth quarter. And, despite the dire budgetary situations of state and local governments, their purchases rose at the fastest pace in more than five years in the second quarter and were basically stable in the third and fourth quarters. This stability almost surely could not have occurred in the absence of the fiscal relief to the states.

The figure also shows the large role of inventory investment in magnifying macroeconomic fluctuations. When the economy goes into a recession, firms want to cut their inventories. As a result, inventory investment moves from its usual slightly positive level to sharply negative, contributing to the fall in output. Then, as firms moderate their inventory reductions, inventory investment rises—that is, becomes less negative— contributing to the recovery of output.

Finally, the turnaround in the automobile industry has been substantial. The Cash for Clunkers program appears to have generated a sharp increase in demand for automobiles in July and August 2009 (Council of Economic Advisers 2009). Sales of light motor vehicles averaged 12.6 million units at an annual rate during these two months, up from an annual rate of 9.6 million units in the second quarter. Although some observers had hypothesized that the July and August sales boost would be offset by a corresponding loss of sales in the months immediately following, sales in September (9.2 million at an annual rate) roughly matched the pace of sales in the first half of 2009, and sales subsequently rebounded to a 10.8 million unit annual pace in the fourth quarter. Employment in motor vehicles and parts hit a low of 633,300 in June 2009 and has increased modestly since then. In December 2009, employment was 655,200.

Both GM and Chrysler proceeded through bankruptcy in an efficient manner, and the new companies emerged far more quickly than outside experts thought would be possible. The companies are performing in line with their restructuring plans, and in November 2009, GM announced its intention to begin repaying the Federal Government earlier than originally expected. It made a first payment of $1 billion in December.

The Labor Market

The ultimate goal of the economic stabilization and recovery policies is to provide a job for every American who seeks one. The recession's impact on the labor market has been severe: employment in December 2009 was 7.2 million below its peak level two years earlier, and the unemployment rate was 10 percent. Moreover, although real GDP has begun to grow, employment losses are continuing.

Nonetheless, there is clear evidence that the labor market is stabilizing. Figure 2-13 shows the average monthly job loss by quarter since 2006. Average monthly job losses have moderated steadily, from a devastating 691,000 in the first quarter of 2009 to 428,000 in the second quarter, 199,000 in the third, and 69,000 in the fourth. The *change* in the average monthly change in employment from the first quarter to the third was the largest over any two-quarter period since 1980, and the change from the first to the fourth quarter was the largest three-quarter change since 1946. Given what we now know about the terrible rate of job loss over the winter, it would have been very difficult for the labor market to stabilize more rapidly than it has.

Figure 2-13
Average Monthly Change in Employment

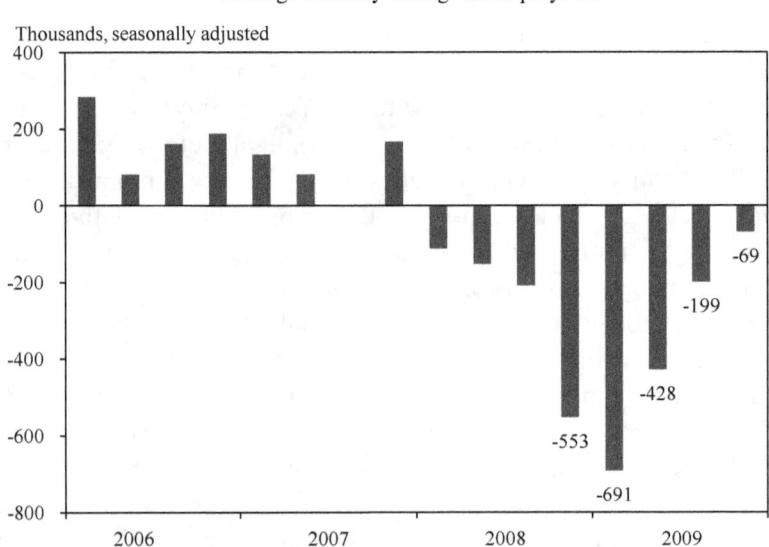

Source: Department of Labor (Bureau of Labor Statistics), Current Employment Statistics survey Series CES0000000001.

One can again use the VAR described earlier to obtain a more refined estimate of how the behavior of employment has differed from its usual pattern. This statistical procedure implies that given the economy's behavior through the first quarter of 2009 and its usual dynamics, one would have expected job losses of about 597,000 per month in the second quarter, 513,000 in the third quarter, and 379,000 in the fourth. Thus, actual employment as of the middle of the second quarter (May) was approximately 300,000 higher than one would have projected given the normal behavior of the economy; as of the middle of the third quarter (August), it was about 1.1 million higher; and as of the middle of the fourth quarter (November), it was about 2.1 million higher. As with the behavior of GDP, the portion of this difference that is attributable to the Recovery Act and other policies cannot be isolated from the portion resulting from other factors. But again, the difference could either understate or overstate the policies' contributions.

As with GDP, economic models can be used to focus specifically on the contributions of the Recovery Act. The results are shown in Figure 2-14. The CEA's multiplier estimates suggest that the Act raised employment relative to what it otherwise would have been by about 400,000 in the second quarter of 2009, 1.1 million in the third quarter, and 1.8 million in the fourth quarter. Again, these estimates are similar to other assessments. For example, CBO's November report estimated that the Act had raised

Figure 2-14
Estimated Effect of the Recovery Act on Employment

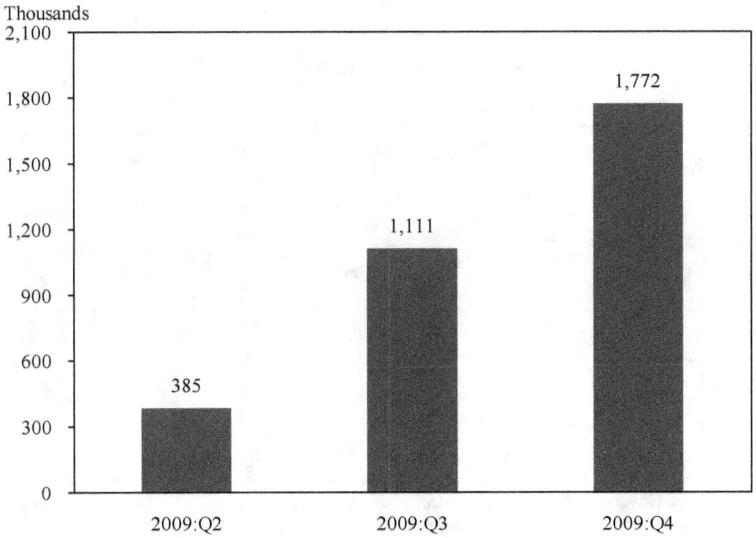

Note: The figure shows the estimated impact on employment relative to what otherwise would have happened.
Source: CEA calculations. See Council of Economic Advisers (2010).

employment in the third quarter by between 0.6 million and 1.6 million, relative to what otherwise would have happened.

A more complete picture of the process of labor market healing can be obtained by looking at labor market indicators beyond employment. Table 2-1 shows some of the main margins along which labor market recovery occurs. The margins are listed from left to right in the rough order in which they tend to adjust coming out of a recession. One of the first margins to respond is productivity—when demand begins to recover or moderates relative to the previous rate of decline, firms initially produce more with the same number of workers. Another early margin is initial claims for unemployment insurance—fewer workers are laid off. A somewhat later margin is the average workweek—firms start increasing production by increasing hours. The usual next step is temporary help employment—when firms decide to hire, they often begin with temporary help. Eventually total employment responds. The unemployment rate usually lags employment slightly because employment growth brings some discouraged workers back into the labor force and because the labor force naturally grows over time. The last item to adjust is usually the duration of unemployment spells, as workers who have been unemployed for extended periods finally find jobs.

The table shows that recovery from this recession is following the typical pattern, with labor market repair evident along the margins that typically respond early in a recovery. Productivity growth has surged as GDP has begun to increase and employment has continued to fall.

Table 2-1
Cyclically Sensitive Elements of Labor Market Adjustment

First to move ———————————▶ Last to move

	Productivity growth, annual rate (percent)	Average monthly change					
		Initial UI claims (thousands/ week)	Workweek (hours)	Temporary help employment (thousands)	Total employment (thousands)	Unemployment rate (percent)	Average duration of unemployment (weeks)
2008:Q4	0.8	22	-0.10	-70	-553	0.39	0.3
2009:Q1	0.3	40	-0.07	-73	-691	0.42	0.4
2009:Q2	6.9	-15	-0.03	-28	-428	0.29	1.2
2009:Q3	8.1ᵖ	-22	0.03	5	-199	0.11	0.7
2009:Q4	7.5ᵉ	-30	0.03	49	-69	0.04	0.9

Notes: This table arranges the indicators according to the order in which they typically first move around business cycle turning points. Quarterly values for the average monthly change are measured from the last month in the previous quarter to the last month in the quarter. p is preliminary; e is estimate.

Sources: Department of Labor (Bureau of Labor Statistics), Series PRS85006092, and Employment Situation Tables A, A-9, and B-1; Department of Labor (Employment and Training Administration).

Initial unemployment insurance claims, which rose precipitously earlier in the recession, have begun to decline at an increasing rate. Likewise, the workweek has gone from shortening to lengthening, albeit slowly. Temporary help employment has changed from extreme declines to substantial increases. So far, total employment has shown a greatly moderating decline but has not yet risen. The pace of increase in the unemployment rate has slowed noticeably, but the unemployment rate has not yet fallen on a quarterly basis. Finally, increases in the duration of unemployment have not yet begun to moderate noticeably.

These data suggest that the labor market is beginning to move in the right direction, but much work remains to be done. The country is not yet seeing the substantial rises in total employment and declines in the unemployment rate that are the ultimate hallmark of robust labor market improvement. And, of course, even once all the indicators are moving solidly in the right direction, the labor market will still have a long way to go before it is fully recovered.

Signs of healing are also beginning to appear in the industrial composition of the stabilization of the labor market. Figure 2-15 shows the average monthly change in each of eight sectors in each of the four quarters of 2009. As one would expect of the beginnings of a recovery from a severe

Figure 2-15
Contributions to the Change in Employment

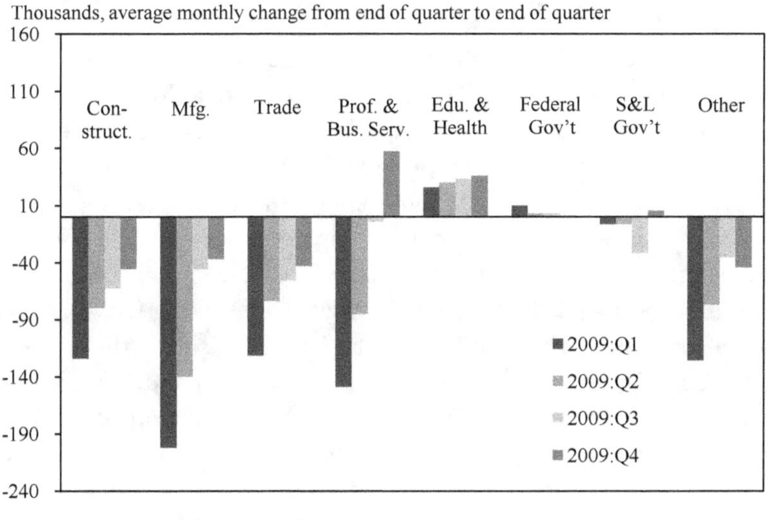

Notes: Bars sum to average monthly change in quarter (-691,000 in Q1; -428,000 in Q2; -199,000 in Q3; -69,000 in Q4). Construct. is construction; Mfg. is manufacturing; Trade is wholesale and retail trade, transportation, and utilities; Prof. & Bus. Serv. is professional and business services; Edu. & Health is education and health; Federal Gov't is Federal Government; S&L Gov't is state and local government.
Source: Department of Labor (Bureau of Labor Statistics), Employment Situation Table B-1.

recession, the moderation in job losses has been particularly pronounced in manufacturing and construction, two of the most cyclically sensitive sectors. There has also been a sharp turnaround in professional business services, driven largely by renewed employment growth in temporary help services.

One area where the Recovery Act appears to have had a direct impact on employment is in state and local government. Despite the enormous harm the recession has done to their budgets, employment in state and local governments has fallen relatively little. Indeed, employment in state and local government, particularly in public education, rose in the fourth quarter.

THE CHALLENGES AHEAD

The financial and economic rescue policies have helped avert an economic calamity and brought about a sharp change in the economy's direction. Output has begun growing again, and employment appears poised to do so as well. But even when the country has returned to a path of steadily growing output and employment, the economy will be far from fully recovered. Since the recession began in December 2007, 7.2 million jobs have been lost. It will take many months of robust job creation to erase that employment deficit. For this reason, it is important to explore policies to speed recovery and spur job creation.

Deteriorating Forecasts

This jobs deficit is much larger than the vast majority of observers anticipated at the end of 2008. This is not the result of a slow economic turn-around. On the contrary, as described above, the change in the economy's direction has been remarkably rapid given the economy's condition in the first quarter of 2009. Rather, the jobs deficit reflects two developments.

The first development is the unanticipated severity of the downturn in the real economy in 2008 and early 2009. Table 2-2 shows consensus fore-casts from November 2008 through February 2009, along with preliminary and actual estimates of real GDP growth. The table shows that the magni-tude of the fall in GDP in the fourth quarter of 2008 and the first quarter of 2009—driven in part by the unexpectedly strong spread of the crisis to the rest of the world—surprised most observers. The Blue Chip Consensus released in mid-December 2008 projected fourth quarter growth would be -4.1 percent and first quarter growth would be -2.4 percent. The actual values turned out to be -5.4 percent and -6.4 percent. The Blue Chip forecast released in mid-January also projected a substantially smaller decline in first quarter real GDP than actually occurred.

Table 2-2
Forecast and Actual Macroeconomic Outcomes

Real GDP Growth					
	2008:Q4	2009:Q1	2009:Q2	2009:Q3	2009:Q4
Blue Chip (11/10/08)	-2.8	-1.5	0.2	1.5	2.1
SPF (11/17/08)	-2.9	-1.1	0.8	0.9	2.3
Blue Chip (12/10/08)	-4.1	-2.4	-0.4	1.2	1.9
Blue Chip (1/10/09)	-5.2	-3.3	-0.8	1.2	2.2
SPF (2/13/09)	--	-5.2	-1.8	1.0	1.8
BEA Advance Estimate	-3.8	-6.1	-1.0	3.5	5.7
BEA Preliminary (2nd) Estimate	-6.2	-5.7	-1.0	2.8	--
Actual	**-5.4**	**-6.4**	**-0.7**	**2.2**	--

Unemployment Rate					
	2008:Q4	2009:Q1	2009:Q2	2009:Q3	2009:Q4
Blue Chip (11/10/08)	6.5	6.9	7.3	7.6	7.7
SPF (11/17/08)	6.6	7.0	7.4	7.6	7.7
Blue Chip (12/10/08)	6.7	7.3	7.7	8.0	8.1
Blue Chip (1/10/09)	6.9	7.4	7.9	8.3	8.4
SPF (2/13/09)	--	7.8	8.3	8.7	8.9
Actual	**6.9**	**8.2**	**9.3**	**9.7**	**10.0**

Notes: In the GDP panel, all numbers are in percent and are seasonally adjusted annual rates. In the unemployment panel, all numbers are in percent and are seasonally adjusted. SPF is the Survey of Professional Forecasters. Dashes indicate data are not available.
Sources: Blue Chip Economic Indicators; Survey of Professional Forecasters; Department of Commerce (Bureau of Economic Analysis), GDP news releases on 1/30/2009, 2/27/2009, 4/29/2009, 5/29/2009, 7/31/2009, 8/27/2009, 10/29/2009, 11/24/2009, 1/29/2010, and National Income and Product Accounts Table 1.1.1, line 1; Department of Labor (Bureau of Labor Statistics), Current Population Survey Series LNS14000000.

Part of the difficulty in forecasting resulted from large data revisions. The official GDP figures available at the end of January 2009 indicated that real GDP had fallen by just 0.2 percent over the four quarters of 2008; revised data now put the decline at 1.9 percent.

The Administration's economic forecast made in January 2009 and released with the fiscal 2010 budget, like the private forecasts, underestimated the speed of GDP decline in the first quarter. It also underestimated average growth over the remaining three quarters of 2009. For the four quarters of 2009, the Administration forecast overall growth of 0.3 percent; the actual value, according to the latest available data, is 0.1 percent.

The second development accounting for the unexpectedly large jobs deficit involves the behavior of the labor market given the behavior of GDP. Table 2-2 also shows consensus forecasts for the unemployment rate. These data indicate that as of December 2008, unemployment in the fourth quarter of 2009 was forecast to be 8.1 percent, dramatically less than the actual value of 10.0 percent. As of mid-January 2009, unemployment was forecast to be 8.4 percent in the fourth quarter. In its forecast made in

January 2009, the Administration unemployment forecast was similar to the consensus forecast.

Some of the unanticipated rise in unemployment was the result of the worse-than-expected GDP growth in 2008 and the beginning of 2009. CEA analysis, however, also suggests that the normal relationship between GDP and unemployment has fit poorly in the current recession. This relationship, termed Okun's law after former CEA Chair Arthur Okun who first identified it, suggests that a fall in GDP of 1 percent relative to its normal trend path is associated with a rise in the unemployment rate of about 0.5 percentage point after four quarters. Figure 2-16 shows the scatter plot of the four-quarter change in real GDP and the four-quarter change in the unemployment rate. The figure shows that although the fit of Okun's law is usually good, the relationship has broken down somewhat during this recession. The error was concentrated in 2009, when the unemployment rate increased considerably faster than might have been expected given the change in real GDP. CEA calculations suggest that as of the fourth quarter of 2009, the unemployment rate was approximately 1.7 percentage points higher than would have been expected given the behavior of real GDP since the business cycle peak in the fourth quarter of 2007.

This unusual rise in the unemployment rate does not appear to result from unusual behavior of the labor force. If anything, the labor force

Figure 2-16
Okun's Law, 2000-2009

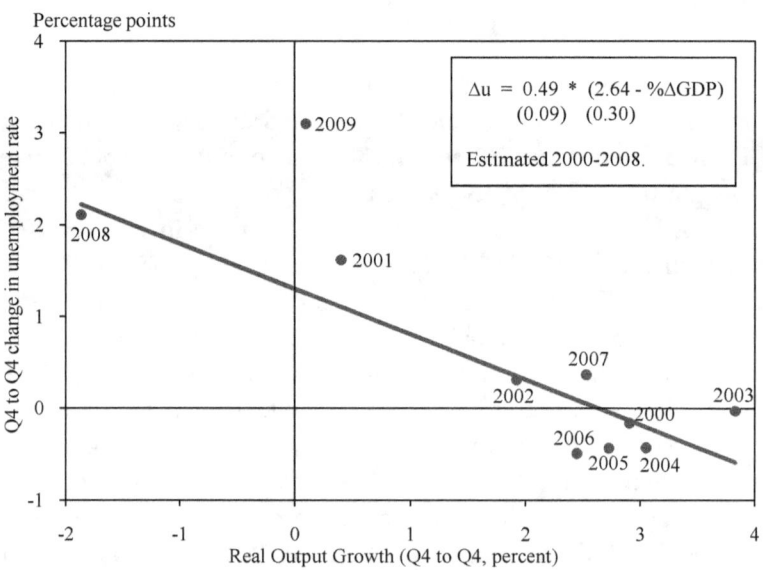

Sources: Department of Commerce (Bureau of Economic Analysis), National Income and Product Accounts Table 1.1.1, line 1; Department of Labor (Bureau of Labor Statistics), Current Population Survey Series LNS11000000 and LNS113000000; CEA calculations.

appears to have contracted somewhat more than usual given the path of the economy. Rather it reflects larger-than-typical falls in employment relative to the decline in GDP. This behavior is consistent with the tremendous increase in productivity during this episode, especially over the final three quarters of 2009. Indeed, labor productivity rose at a 6.9 percent annual rate in the second quarter and at an 8.1 percent rate in the third quarter; if productivity rose by a similar amount in the fourth quarter, as seems likely, the increase will have been one of the fastest over three quarters in postwar history.

The Administration Forecast

Looking forward, the Administration projects steady but moderate GDP growth over the near and medium term. Table 2-3 reports the Administration's forecast used in preparing the President's fiscal year 2011 budget. The table shows that GDP growth in 2010 is forecast to be 3 percent.

Table 2-3
Administration Economic Forecast

	Nominal GDP	Real GDP (chain-type)	GDP price index (chain-type)	Con-sumer price index (CPI-U)	Un-employ-ment rate (percent)	Interest rate, 91-day Treasury bills (percent)	Interest rate, 10-year Treasury notes (percent)	Nonfarm payroll employ-ment (average monthly change, Q4 to Q4, thou-sands)
	Percent change, Q4 to Q4				Level, calendar year			
2008 (actual)	0.1	-1.9	1.9	1.5	5.8	1.4	3.7	-189
2009	0.4	-0.5	0.9	1.4	9.3	0.2	3.3	-419
2010	4.0	3.0	1.0	1.3	10.0	0.4	3.9	95
2011	5.7	4.3	1.4	1.7	9.2	1.6	4.5	190
2012	6.1	4.3	1.7	2.0	8.2	3.0	5.0	251
2013	6.0	4.2	1.7	2.0	7.3	4.0	5.3	274
2014	5.7	3.9	1.7	2.0	6.5	4.1	5.3	267
2015	5.2	3.4	1.7	2.0	5.9	4.1	5.3	222
2016	5.0	3.1	1.8	2.1	5.5	4.1	5.3	181
2017	4.5	2.7	1.8	2.1	5.3	4.1	5.3	139
2018	4.5	2.6	1.8	2.1	5.2	4.1	5.3	113
2019	4.4	2.5	1.8	2.1	5.2	4.1	5.3	98
2020	4.3	2.5	1.8	2.1	5.2	4.1	5.3	93

Notes: Based on data available as of November 18, 2009. Interest rate on 91-day Treasury bills is measured on a secondary market discount basis. The figures do not reflect the upcoming BLS benchmark revision, which is expected to reduce 2008 and 2009 job growth by a cumulative 824,000 jobs.
Sources: CEA calculations; Department of Commerce (Bureau of Economic Analysis and Economics and Statistics Administration); Department of Labor (Bureau of Labor Statistics); Department of the Treasury; Office of Management and Budget.

The Administration estimates that normal or potential GDP growth will be roughly 2½ percent per year (see Box 2-1). Because projected GDP growth is only slightly stronger than potential growth, relatively little decline is projected in the unemployment rate during 2010. Indeed, it is possible that the rate will rise for a while as some discouraged workers return to the labor force, before starting to generally decline. Consistent with this, employment growth is projected to be roughly equal to normal trend growth of about 100,000 per month.

Box 2-1: Potential Real GDP Growth

The Administration forecast is based on the idea that real GDP fluctuates around a potential level that trends upward at a relatively steady rate. Over the budget window, potential real GDP is projected to grow at a 2.5 percent annual rate. Potential real GDP growth is a measure of the sustainable rate of growth of productive capacity.

The growth rate of the economy over the long run is determined by its supply side components, which include population, labor force participation, the ratio of nonfarm business employment to household employment, the length of the workweek, and labor productivity. The Administration's forecast for the contribution of the growth rates of these supply side factors to potential real GDP growth is shown in the accompanying table.

Components of Potential Real GDP Growth, 2009-2020

Component	Contribution (Percentage points)
Civilian noninstitutional population aged 16+	1.0
Labor force participation rate	-0.3
Employment rate	0.0
Ratio of nonfarm business employment to household employment	-0.0
Average weekly hours (nonfarm business)	-0.1
Output per hour (productivity, nonfarm business)	2.3
Ratio of real GDP to nonfarm business output	-0.4
SUM: Real GDP	2.5

Note: All contributions are in percentage points at an annual rate.
Sources: CEA calculations; Department of the Treasury; Office of Management and Budget.

Over the next 11 years, the working-age population is projected to grow 1.0 percent per year, the rate projected by the Census Bureau.

Continued on next page

Box 2-1, continued

The normal or potential labor force participation rate, which fell at a 0.3 percent annual rate during the past 8 years, is expected to continue declining at that pace. The continued projected decline results from the aging baby boom generation entering their retirement years. The potential employment rate (that is, 1 minus the normal or potential unemployment rate) is not expected to contribute to potential GDP growth because no change is anticipated in the unemployment rate consistent with stable inflation. The potential ratio of nonfarm business employment to household employment is also expected to be flat during the forecast horizon—consistent with its average behavior in the long run. This would be a change, however, from its puzzling 0.5 percent annual rate of decline during the past business cycle. The potential workweek is projected to edge down slightly (0.1 percent per year). This is a slightly shallower pace of decline than over the past 50 years, when it declined 0.3 percent per year. Over the 11-year projection interval, some firming of the workweek would be a natural labor market accommodation to the anticipated decline in labor force participation.

Potential growth of labor productivity is projected at 2.3 percent per year, a conservative forecast relative to its measured product-side growth rate (2.8 percent) between the past two business cycle peaks, but close to an alternative income-side measure of productivity growth (2.2 percent) during the same period. The ratio of real GDP to nonfarm business output is expected to continue to subtract from overall growth as it has over most long periods, because the nonfarm business sector generally grows faster than other sectors, such as government, households, and nonprofit institutions. Together, the sum of all of the components is the growth rate of potential real GDP, which is 2.5 percent per year.

As Table 2-3 shows, actual real GDP is projected to grow more rapidly than potential real GDP over most of the forecast horizon. The most important reason for the difference is that the actual employment rate is projected to rise as millions of workers who are currently unemployed return to employment and so contribute to GDP growth.

Traditionally, the large amount of slack would be expected to put substantial downward pressure on wage and price inflation. For this reason, inflation is projected to remain low in 2010. However, because inflationary expectations remain well anchored, inflation is not likely to slow dramatically or become negative (that is, turn into deflation).

In 2011, slightly higher GDP growth of approximately 4 percent is projected (again measured from fourth quarter to fourth quarter). Consistent with this, stronger employment growth and a more substantial decline in the unemployment rate are expected in 2011. However, because GDP growth is still not projected to be as robust as that following some other deep recessions, continued large output gaps are anticipated. This will limit the upward movement of the inflation rate toward a pace consistent with the Federal Reserve's long-term target inflation rate of about 2 percent. Moreover, employment growth is unlikely to be large enough to reduce the employment shortfall dramatically in 2011.

Responsible Policies to Spur Job Creation

This large employment gap and the prospects that it is likely to recede only slowly make a compelling case for additional measures to spur private sector job creation. The Administration is therefore exploring a range of possibilities and working with Congress to pass measures into law.

Several principles are guiding this process. First, at a time when the budget deficit is large and the country faces significant long-run fiscal challenges, measures must be cost-effective. Second, given that the employment consequences of the recession have been severe, measures must focus particularly on job creation. And third, measures must be tailored to the state of the economy: the policies that are appropriate when an economy is contracting rapidly may not be the same as those that are appropriate for an economy that is growing again but operating below capacity.

Guided by these principles, the Administration has identified three key priorities. One is a multifaceted program to jump-start job creation by small businesses, which are critical to growth and have been particularly harmed by the recession. Among the possible policies in this area are investment incentives, tax incentives for hiring, and additional steps to increase the availability of loans backed by the Small Business Administration. These policies may be particularly effective at a time when the economy is growing—so that the question for many firms is not whether to hire but when—and at a time when credit availability remains an important constraint.

Initiatives to encourage energy efficiency and clean energy are another priority. One proposal involves incentives for homeowners to retrofit their homes for energy efficiency. Because in many cases the effect of such incentives would be to lead homeowners to make cost-saving investments earlier than they otherwise would have, they might have an especially large impact. In addition, the employment effects would be concentrated in construction, an area that has been particularly hard-hit by the recession.

The Administration has also supported extending tax credits through the Department of Energy that promote the manufacture of advanced energy products and providing incentives to increase the energy efficiency of public and nonprofit buildings.

A third priority is infrastructure investment. The experience of the Recovery Act suggests that spending on infrastructure is an effective way to put people back to work while creating lasting investments that raise future productivity. For this reason, the Administration is supporting an additional investment of up to $50 billion in roads, bridges, airports, transit, rail, and water projects. Funneling some of these funds through programs such as the Transportation Investment Generating Economic Recovery (TIGER) program at the Department of Transportation, which is a competitive grant program, could offer a way to ensure that the projects with the highest returns receive top priority.

Finally, it is critical to maintain our support for the individuals and families most affected by the recession by extending the emergency funding for such programs as unemployment insurance and health insurance subsidies for the unemployed. This support not only cushions the worst effects of the downturn, but also boosts spending and so spurs job creation. Similarly, it is important to maintain support for state and local governments. The budgets of these governments remain under severe strain, and many are cutting back in anticipation of fiscal year 2011 deficits. Additional fiscal support could therefore have a rapid impact on spending, and would do so by maintaining crucial services and preventing harmful tax increases.

CONCLUSION

The recession that began at the end of 2007 became the "Great Recession" following the financial crisis in the fall of 2008. In the wake of the collapse of Lehman Brothers in September, American families faced devastating job losses, high unemployment, scarce credit, and lost wealth. Late 2008 and 2009 will be remembered as a time of great trial for American workers, businesses, and families.

But 2009 should also be remembered as a year when even more tragic losses and dislocation did not occur. As terrible as this recession has been, a second Great Depression would have been far worse. Had policymakers not responded as aggressively as they did to shore up the financial system, maintain demand, and provide relief to those directly harmed by the downturn, the outcome could have been much more dire.

As 2010 begins, there are strong signs that the American economy is starting to recover. Housing and financial markets appear to have stabilized and real GDP is growing again. The labor market also appears to be healing, showing the expected early pattern of response to output expansion.

With millions of Americans still unemployed, much work remains to restore the American economy to health. It will take a prolonged and robust GDP expansion to eliminate the large jobs deficit that has opened up over the course of the recession. Only when the unemployment rate has returned to normal levels and families are once again secure in their jobs, homes, and savings will this terrible recession truly be over.

REFERENCES

Almeida, Heitor, et al. 2009. "Corporate Debt Maturity and the Real Effects of the 2007 Credit Crisis." Working Paper 14990. Cambridge, MA: National Bureau of Economic Research (May).

Bernanke, Ben S. 1983. "Nonmonetary Effects of the Financial Crisis in the Propagation of the Great Depression." *American Economic Review* 73, no. 3: 257–76.

Broda, Christian, and Jonathan Parker. 2008. "The Impact of the 2008 Tax Rebates on Consumer Spending: Preliminary Evidence." Working Paper. University of Chicago, Graduate School of Business (July).

Campello, Murillo, John Graham, and Campbell R. Harvey. 2009. "The Real Effects of Financial Constraints: Evidence from a Financial Crisis." Working Paper 15552. Cambridge, MA: National Bureau of Economic Research (December).

Congressional Budget Office. 2009a. "Estimated Impact of the American Recovery and Reinvestment Act on Employment and Economic Output as of September 2009." November.

———. 2009b. Letter to the Honorable Charles E. Grassley. "Estimated Macroeconomic Impacts of the American Recovery and Reinvestment Act of 2009." March 2.

Council of Economic Advisers. 2009. "Economic Analysis of the Car Allowance Rebate System ('Cash for Clunkers')." September.

———. 2010. "The Economic Impact of the American Recovery and Reinvestment Act of 2009." Second Quarterly Report to Congress. January.

Gertler, Mark, and Simon Gilchrist. 1994. "Monetary Policy, Business Cycles, and the Behavior of Small Manufacturing Firms." *Quarterly Journal of Economics* 109, no. 2: 309–40.

Kashyap, Anil K, Owen A. Lamont, and Jeremy C. Stein. 1994. "Credit Conditions and the Cyclical Behavior of Inventories." *Quarterly Journal of Economics* 109, no. 3: 565–92.

Lamont, Owen A. 1997. "Cash Flow and Investment: Evidence from Internal Capital Markets." *Journal of Finance* 52, no. 1: 83–109.

Peek, Joe, and Eric S. Rosengren. 2000. "Collateral Damage: Effects of the Japanese Bank Crisis on Real Activity in the United States." *American Economic Review* 90, no. 1: 30–45.

Rauh, Joshua D. 2006. "Investment and Financing Constraints: Evidence from the Funding of Corporate Pension Plans." *Journal of Finance* 61, no. 1: 33–71.

Rudebusch, Glenn D. 2009. "The Fed's Monetary Policy Response to the Current Crisis." FRBSF Economic Letter 2009-17. Federal Reserve Bank of San Francisco (May).

Sahm, Claudia R., Matthew D. Shapiro, and Joel B. Slemrod. 2009. "Household Response to the 2008 Tax Rebate: Survey Evidence and Aggregate Implications." Working Paper 15421. Cambridge, MA: National Bureau of Economic Research (October).

Shiller, Robert J. 2005. *Irrational Exuberance*. 2nd ed. Princeton University Press.